STRESS-PROOF
your
HEART

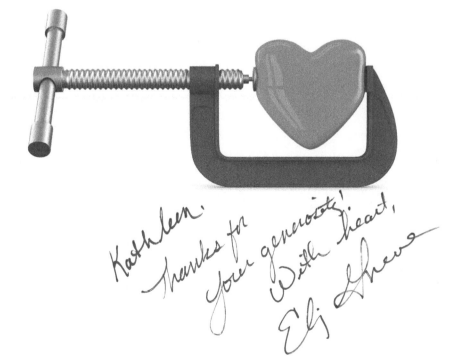

Kathleen,
Thanks for
your generosity!
With heart,
Elj Greeve

LIVE LONGER, FEEL BETTER, AND PROTECT YOUR HEALTH

STRESS-PROOF
— *your* —
HEART

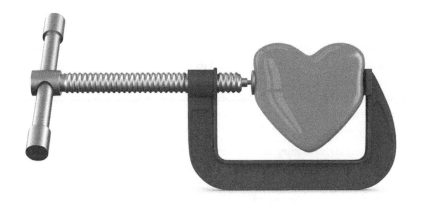

ELIZ GREENE
LOW STRESS & GREAT SUCCESS

Published and Distributed by
SOUND WISDOM
PO Box 310
Shippensburg, PA 17257-0310
717-530-2122
info@soundwisdom.com
www.soundwisdom.com

Cover/Jacket designer Eileen Rockwell

ISBN 13 TP: 978-1-64095-163-1

ISBN 13 eBook: 978-1-64095-164-8

For Worldwide Distribution, Printed in the U.S.A.

2 3 4 5 6 / 23 22 21 20

A note about
the people in this book:

In my work, I have the privilege of hearing stories from audience members, study participants, people I interview, and through comments on my blog and social media. Common themes of the impact of stress emerged over time in these stories. Those themes are represented by the characters in this book. Any resemblance to actual persons, living or dead, or actual events is purely coincidental.

This book is not intended as a substitute for the medical advice of physicians. You should regularly consult a physician in matters relating to your health, especially if you have symptoms of heart disease, heart attack, or stroke.

For Clay, Grace, and Callie –
you are my whole world.

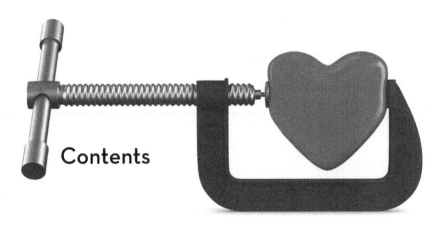

Contents

Why Stress-Proof Your Heart?

A stress-proof heart is strong enough to get you to the moments you don't want to miss.

Keeping my heart strong and protecting it from stress aren't abstract ideas for me—they're literally life-or-death skills. When I was 35 years old and seven months pregnant with twins, I had a massive heart attack. Fortunately, I was already in a great hospital on bed rest due to pre-term labor. In the matter of a few hours, my life changed dramatically. A ten-minute cardiac arrest stopped my heart and my breathing. Doctors were able to use a defibrillator to get my heart started again, but our day wasn't over yet. My beautiful daughters were delivered by Caesarian section—seven weeks early—and I underwent five hours of open-heart surgery.

The surgeon repaired my heart, but a small part of it doesn't beat anymore. Even though my pregnancy caused the heart attack, I am at a higher risk of having another, so controlling my risk factors is essential. I can control my diet and be physically active, but stress is an exponential multiplier of risk I simply can't afford. To reduce my heightened risk of having another heart attack, I've spent the 17 years since then honing practical and implementable strategies to manage stress for myself and the thousands of audience members and readers I reach each year.

I know that merely having information rarely changes behavior. My recovery was fueled by the motivation to see our daughters grow up. My husband, Clay, and I have watched our girls grow from scrawny premature babies into strong, smart, amazing young women, and I can't wait to see what they do next. Real change becomes possible only when we connect information to something we hold dear. What keeps me up at night is the thought of not being here for my family's important moments. I was given the gift of a heart attack at age 35, and I know if I want to see my girls graduate from college, I have to protect my heart from stress.

Some stress is natural; too much is a problem

We can't alleviate all stress, and we wouldn't want to even if we could. Some stress is natural and necessary; it is what gives us the zing of energy to get things done. The zing is the result of the hormone cortisol flooding the system when the body detects danger or stress. Cortisol quickens reactions, increases pulse and blood pressure, and even thickens the blood (to prevent bleeding to death in case of injury).

Trouble comes when that zing becomes a constant thrum, continually triggering the cortisol response rather than allowing it to ebb and flow as we need it. Thicker blood, higher blood pressure, and increased pulse all make the heart work harder, which is why prolonged high stress doubles the risk of heart attack and stroke. Chronic high cortisol levels also result in unpleasant physical symptoms, including weight gain (especially in the face and belly), muscle weakness, and mood swings, depression, or irritability.

The stress-proof mission

For nearly two decades, I've traveled the country speaking about stress, heart health, and wellness. Without fail, after a speech, an audience member will approach me to share the struggle to find work-life balance and manage stress. One such audience member, Linda, stands out in my memory.

Linda's children are adults now, and she works long hours as the CFO of a company. She tries to exercise, takes a yoga class, and does all of the typical time management and goal-setting work-life balance remedies, but nothing is working. She is overworked, overtired, overweight, and just plain over work-life balance.

She's not alone. Inspired by people like Linda and recognizing stress as an essential and often under-addressed risk factor, I conducted a research study on job stress. I surveyed more than 4,000 workers around the world, across a variety of industries.

I initially conducted this research to quantify the problem of work-life imbalance and create better stress-management strategies. I was shocked by what I learned.

- 💜 Work-life balance strategies, no matter how creative, thoughtful, and well researched, are addressing the wrong problem.
- 💜 The vast majority of my respondents said that their stress was caused by overwhelm and uncertainty.
- 💜 Most stress is caused by issues outside of people's control, such as downsizing, managerial issues, or change.

Why this book?

I wrote *Stress-Proof Your Heart* as a guide for people like Linda and the other people you'll meet in this book who are dealing with unrelenting stress caused by overwhelm and uncertainty. The assessments, strategies, and tools are designed to evaluate the physical impact of stress and then offset that impact to protect your heart.

This book has two sections. The first uses a series of assessments to evaluate the physical impact of your stress. The second section provides a bank of strategies to offset the physical impact of your stress.

My hope is that you will use this book to be able to withstand high stress, change, crisis, and to bounce back from illness—because you deserve a fulfilling and enjoyable life.

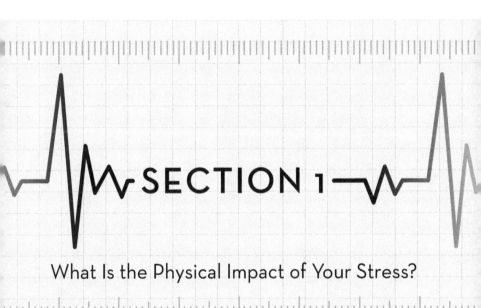

SECTION 1

What Is the Physical Impact of Your Stress?

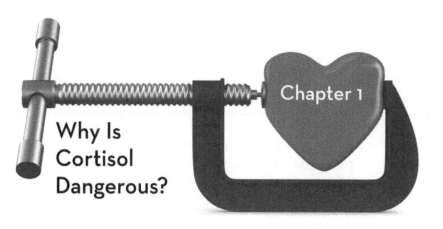

Why Is Cortisol Dangerous?

Chapter 1

Jerome thought he was just tired. He has good reason to be. The last couple of years have been busy, having started a law firm with some friends. As the managing partner, his hours are long. He began experiencing spells of dizziness, during which he worried about passing out. He couldn't afford to look weak in front of clients—or worse, opposing counsel—so he went to the urgent care clinic. Of course, the doctor ordered a bunch of tests. Jerome figured she'd tell him to start exercising more and eat better.

He wasn't expecting to be told he had blockage in two of the arteries in his heart. He couldn't believe it. He needed to have stents put in. He was only 47, and he needed a heart procedure. He really tries to eat well and get some exercise. He isn't overweight. Maybe all the long hours and stress took more of a toll than he thought?

Jerome is right to wonder about the impact of stress on heart health. As mentioned in the introduction, high levels of the stress hormone cortisol cause thicker blood, higher blood pressure, and increased pulse, which all make the heart work harder. Prolonged high stress weakens the heart and doubles the risk of heart attack and stroke.

Chronic high cortisol levels also result in unpleasant physical symptoms, including weight gain (especially in the face and belly), muscle weakness, and mood swings, depression, or irritability. In addition, high cortisol levels are related to the increased risk of cancer and heart disease, along with other conditions of the endocrine and immune systems. Heart disease, however, is the number-one cause of death for women and men of all ages. In fact, more people die of heart disease than the next seven causes, including all kinds of cancer, combined.

Like Jerome, many relatively younger people find themselves diagnosed with coronary artery disease, heart rhythm issues, or with high risk factors such as elevated blood pressure, cholesterol, or blood sugar.

That is the bad news.

The good news is that your body is naturally equipped to process cortisol out of your system if you let it.

A stress-proof person more effectively processes the cortisol, reducing it to normal levels, which in turn protects the heart, helps the person feel better, and even allows the brain to function better.

Evaluating the impact that stress creates on your physical health is essential to reducing it.

How Stressed Are You?

Chapter 2

Chantel sits in her car watching the time of arrival to her meeting tick by. She is going to be late, which is not the first impression she wanted to make with her new design client. Editing the proposal kept her up well past midnight. In fact, she can't remember the last time she went to sleep the same day she woke up. She feels terrible for nearly taking her assistant's head off this morning, but she just doesn't seem to have any patience left. As traffic starts to clear, she pops a couple of antacids to calm her stomach and takes a deep breath. Maybe she'll still get there in time.

The effects of stress show up sometimes in subtle symptoms—irritability, stomach upset, and sleeplessness, for example. But it is often challenging to quantify stress. I developed a Stress Level Index as part of my research on job stress. The result of this index indicates how likely it is that your stress will impact your physical health.

Your level—mild, moderate, critical, or acute—is used in the assessment tool to calculate your physical stress impact. This impact is a clear measure of how much danger is caused by your stress level.

THE STRESS LEVEL INDEX

Think about a typical week. Use the worksheet on page 22 to keep track of how often you experience the things described below. Simply put an "X" in the appropriate space for each statement.

How often (never, some of the time, about half of the time, most of the time, or always) do you experience the following:

- Feeling overwhelmed by the number of things to be done in the time allowed
- Sleeping less than seven hours at night
- Taking on tasks because others aren't doing them or aren't doing them well enough
- Skipping a meal or grabbing something unhealthy because you are too busy
- Worrying something will "fall through the cracks"
- Feeling unable to prioritize because there is too much to do
- Neglecting important things or people
- Missing out on activities you enjoy

💜 Having trouble falling asleep because you are thinking about what needs to be done or about an uncertain future

💜 Dwelling on mistakes or things left undone

💜 Taking on tasks to protect other people's balance, reputation, or job

💜 Worrying about making a mistake

💜 Feeling angry or frustrated about something your boss did (or didn't) do

💜 Feeling annoyed, distracted, or "dumped on" by a co-worker

💜 Worrying about your health

💜 Feeling concerned about money

💜 Spending time at work thinking about personal issues

💜 Spending time at home thinking about work issues

Stress Level Index Worksheet

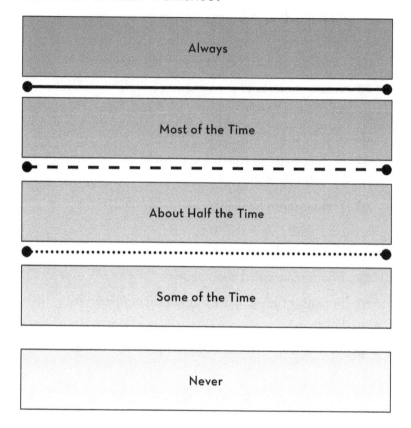

Always

Most of the Time

About Half the Time

Some of the Time

Never

UNDERSTANDING YOUR STRESS LEVEL INDEX RESULTS

Look at where your marks are clustered on the worksheet in relation to the three lines.

Where are your marks?	Stress Level Index
Most marks below the dotted line	Mild
Most marks between the dotted line and the dashed line	Moderate
Most marks between the dashed line and the solid line	Critical
Most marks above the dashed line	Acute

If your Stress Level Index is moderate, critical, or acute, it is likely that your physical health is at risk. To understand the degree of that impact, please complete the Physical Stress Impact Assessment found in Chapter 3.

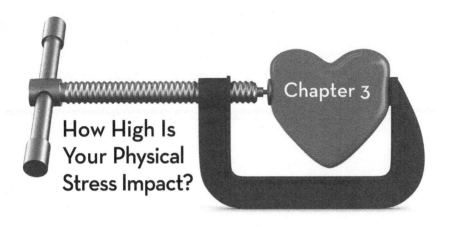

How High Is Your Physical Stress Impact?

Chapter 3

For almost two decades, I've traveled the country encouraging people to pay attention to a topic most of us would like to ignore—heart health. As a professional speaker, I've had to come up with creative ways of capturing people's attention and compelling them to think about their hearts. We all know heart health is important, but it isn't a sexy, must-have topic at most conferences.

One of the most difficult things to explain is how risk factors don't just add up; they multiply exponentially.

Think about it like this: stress is the Power Ball of risk factors. It makes your risk exponentially higher. This Power Ball effect is your physical stress impact.

How do you determine the physical impact of your stress, or the size of your Power Ball? I developed the assessment in this chapter based on information from the American Heart Association and the American College of Cardiology. Thousands of clients and audience members have used this assessment to determine their personal risk of heart disease.

The results of the assessment demonstrate the impact of stress on your health. Don't worry, in Section 2 you'll learn how to offset your physical stress impact by helping your body return your cortisol level back to normal.

PHYSICAL STRESS IMPACT ASSESSMENT

Imagine you've been given 100 chances to live to the ripe old age of 97 in excellent health, with all of your faculties intact, and then pass away peacefully in your sleep. Sounds great, right? Those chances are represented by circles on the worksheet on page 47 in Chapter 4. Risk factors for heart disease, including stress, take away some of those chances.

In this chapter, you'll find a series of questions about risk factors. As you answer the questions on the following pages, you will be instructed to cross off some of those circles, representing lost chances of that long, healthy life.

Some risk factors, like stress, are risk-multipliers, which exponentially increase the number of chances you may lose, so it is important to take this quiz in order. The results of the later questions depend on the answers in the first sections.

After you complete the quiz, you will have a graphic illustration of your risk of heart disease by evaluating three categories of risk:

- Inherited risk factors
- Internal risk factors
- Lifestyle risk factors

The results will help identify steps you can take to offset the physical impact of your stress.

1. ## Inherited Risk Factors: Some risk factors are yours for keeps

There are certain risk factors we can't change; we are born with them. Age, gender, ethnicity, and family history all lay the foundation for our physical health and heart disease risk.

Your Age and Gender:

Women initially enjoy some protection thanks to estrogen, but that advantage decreases with age. At age 65, the risk for men and women equals out.

Cross out all circles that apply to you.

Are you age 44 or younger?

Keep your circles.

Are you using hormonal birth control such as the pill, ring, or patch (any age)?

Cross out 5 circles.

Are you a woman age 45–65 and still menstruating regularly?

Cross out 5 circles.

Are you age 45–65 and peri- or post-menopausal?

Cross out 7 circles.

Are you age 65 or older?

Cross out 10 circles.

Number of circles to cross out
for your age and gender: _____

Your Ethnicity:

People from some areas of the world are genetically predisposed to experience more heart disease.

Cross out all circles that apply to you.

Is your family from Hawaii or India?

Cross out **10** circles.

Is your family from Mexico?

Cross out **10** circles.

Is your family from Africa?

Cross out **10** circles.

Is your family Native American or Native Alaskan?

Cross out **10** circles.

Number of circles to cross out
for your ethnicity: _____

Your Family History:

Your close biological relatives' health provides a look into your future. Even if you do not have symptoms today, a strong family history of heart disease can lead you and your doctor to implement treatment to prevent or slow down the development of heart disease.

Take a look at the health of your close relatives. Your parents, siblings, grandparents, aunts, and uncles may be experiencing heart disease symptoms that they have not shared with you. If you are diagnosed with heart disease, share the information with your family so that they can be checked as well.

Cross out all circles that apply to you.

Has your mother, father, or a sibling been diagnosed with heart disease before age 60?

Cross out **10** circles.

Has a grandfather, grandmother, uncle, or aunt been diagnosed with heart disease before age 60 or died of a heart attack or stroke?

Cross out **10** circles.

Have you had a heart attack or been diagnosed with heart disease?

Cross out **20** circles.

Don't know your family history?

Cross out 5 circles.

Number of circles to cross out
for your family history: _____

Total number of circles to cross out
for your inherited risk factors: _____

Go to the worksheet on page 47 to record your inherited risk factors results like this:

Example Stress Burden Assessment Worksheet – Internal Risk Factors

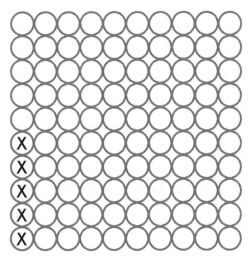

2. Internal Risk Factors: Some risk factors are silent

Internal risk factors don't typically have symptoms, especially in their early stages, but they can drastically increase your risk of developing heart disease. These risk factors need to be evaluated by a health professional.

Your Blood Pressure:

About one in every three Americans has high blood pressure. There are no symptoms, and only just over half of the people with high blood pressure receive treatment.

Often called the "silent killer," uncontrolled high blood pressure can cause stroke, heart attack, heart failure, and kidney failure.

Blood pressure measures how hard your heart needs to work to push your blood through the veins and arteries. The top number is the pressure during a heartbeat, and the bottom number is the pressure between beats.

For this quiz, we'll keep it simple and look at the top number.

Is your top number 119 or lower?

Keep your circles.

Is your top number between 120 and 139?

Cross out 5 circles.

Is your top number between 140 and 159?

Cross out **15** circles.

Is your top number above 160?

Cross out 25 circles.

Number of circles to cross out
for your blood pressure level: _____

Your Cholesterol Level:

Cholesterol is a fatty substance that travels through the bloodstream and is essential to our health. "Good" cholesterol, high-density lipoprotein (HDL), carries our hormones and even keeps our skin supple.

But too much cholesterol, especially low-density lipoprotein (LDL)—the "bad" kind—is a problem. Along the way, this "bad" cholesterol can deposit and sink into the walls of arteries, creating a buildup called plaque. Think of it as sludge forming on the inside of pipes.

As plaque builds, the artery walls thicken, which narrows the space available for blood to flow. Ultimately, the buildup of plaque slows down the flow of blood. This reduced blood flow robs cells of the oxygen they need. This type of heart disease, atherosclerosis, is often referred to as "hardening of the arteries."

When these plaque deposits are in arteries that supply the heart, it is called coronary artery disease. When they form in the arteries that supply the arms and legs, it is called peripheral artery disease.

Is your HDL:

Below 40?

Cross out 5 circles.

40 or above?

Keep your circles.

Is your LDL:

Below 100?

Keep your circles.

100 to 129?

Cross out **5** circles.

130 to 159?

Cross out **10** circles.

160 to 189?

Cross out **20** circles.

190 or above?

Cross out **30** circles.

Are your triglycerides:

149 or lower?

Keep your circles.

150 to 199?

Cross out **5** circles.

200 to 499?

Cross out **10** circles.

500 or above?

Cross out **25** circles.

Number of circles to cross out
for your cholesterol level: _____

Your Blood Sugar:

A blood sugar test measures the amount of glucose present in your system. Glucose is the fuel needed for your body to run. As you digest food, your body produces glucose to feed your cells. Your pancreas then releases insulin, which signals to your body that it is time to absorb the glucose. If your body doesn't produce enough insulin, the glucose stays in your bloodstream and causes trouble. High blood sugar levels can permanently damage the pancreas and cause the type of heart disease marked by the hardening of the arteries.

For simplicity, this quiz uses the most common type of blood sugar test, the fasting plasma glucose test.

Is your fasting glucose level:

100 or below?

    Keep your circles.

101–125?

    Cross out **10** circles.

125 or above?

Double the number of circles crossed out.(Count the number of circles currently crossed out and then cross that number off again.)

Number of circles to cross out
for your blood sugar level: _____

Total number of circles to cross out for your internal risk factors: _____

Go to the worksheet on page 47 to record your inherited risk factors results like this:

Example Stress Burden Assessment Worksheet – Internal Risk Factors

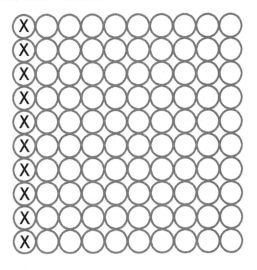

3. Lifestyle Risk Factors: Some risk factors are within your control

Our activity level, what we eat, our habits, how much we sleep, and how much we worry impacts risk considerably. Lifestyle risk factors exponentially amplify risk. These are risk factors that we control and have the most potential to improve.

Waist-to-Hip Ratio:

Your body shape is a clue to your risk. The waist-to-hip ratio is a simple, and in many ways more helpful than BMI, measurement to determine how weight is distributed. Where you carry fat is important. Fat that is around the muscle and bone in your hips and legs is fine. Fat around the organs in your abdomen is dangerous.

Follow these easy steps to determine your waist-to-hip ratio:

1. Find a tape measure—the more flexible, the better.
2. Find your belly button.
3. Wrap the tape measure around your waist at the level of your belly button.
4. Record your waist measurement below.
5. Find the widest part between your hip bone and the top of your knees.
6. Wrap the tape measure around that point.
7. Record your hip measurement below.

8. Divide your waist measurement by your hip measurement (WM ÷ HM).

9. The resulting number tells you the percentage your waist measurement is compared to your hip measurement. (For example, 0.7 is 70 percent.)

Waist Measurement (WM): _____

Hip Measurement (HM): _____

Understanding Your Waist-to-Hip Results:

Men:

The healthy ratio for men is 1 or 100 percent. In other words, for men the hips and waist should measure the same. They should be straight at the torso rather than round.

Women:

The healthy ratio for men is 0.8 or 80 percent. In other words, for women the hips should be about 20 percent bigger than the waist. They should be curvy at the torso rather than round.

Waist-to-Hip Results

Waist-to-Hip	Impact on Risk
Men 1 or less Women .8 or less	Stays the Same
Men greater than 1 Women greater than .8	Double (Count the number of circles currently crossed out and then cross that number off again)

Number of circles to cross out
for your waist-to-hip results: _____

Smoking:

Smoking is the fast track to heart disease. People who smoke get heart disease decades before people who do not smoke.

Smoking Results

Smoking	Impact on Risk
Non-smoker	Stays the Same
Live or Work with Smoker	Double (Count the number of circles currently crossed out and then cross that number off again)
Smoker	Triple (Count the number of circles currently crossed out, multiply it by 2, and then cross that number off)

Number of circles to cross out
for your smoking results: _____

Total number of circles to cross out
for your lifestyle risk factors: _____

Go to the worksheet on page 47 to record your inherited risk factors results like this:

Example Stress Burden Assessment Worksheet –
Lifestyle Risk Factors

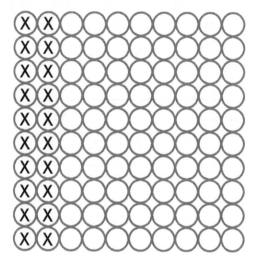

Your Stress:

Stress has an insidious impact on heart health. The physical changes in the body caused by stress magnify risk. Use the results of the Stress Level Index to evaluate the impact on your risk.

Stress Results

Stress Level Index	Impact on Risk
Mild	Stays the Same
Moderate	Increase number by half (Count the number of circles currently crossed out, divide by 2, and cross out that number)
Critical	Double (Count the number of circles currently crossed out and then cross that number off again)
Acute	Triple (Count the number of circles currently crossed out, multiply it by 2, and then cross that number off)

Rather than crossing these circles out on the worksheet on page 47, write an "S" in them. The circles marked with an "S" indicate the physical impact of your stress.

Number of circles in which to write "S": _____

Example Stress Burden Assessment Worksheet – Stress

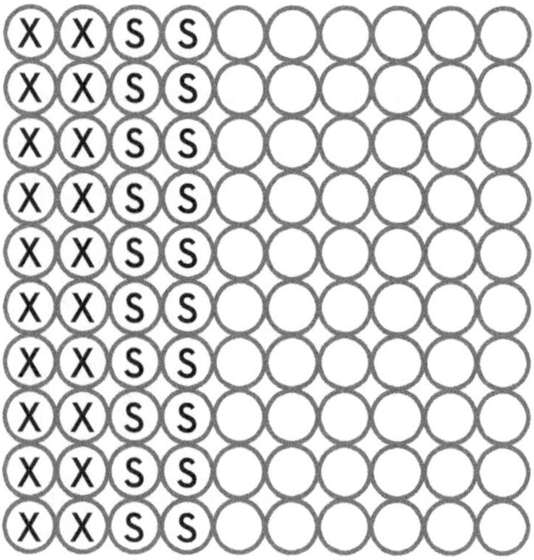

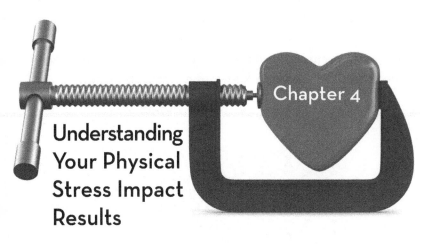

Understanding Your Physical Stress Impact Results

Chapter 4

"You need to get a handle on your stress," the doctor said. Charlene scoffed to herself, thinking that was easier said than done. As the regional sales director for a pharmaceutical company, she is constantly on the road. Keeping her team focused and up to date on changes is a non-stop struggle. She just lost one team member to another company, and finding a good replacement seems impossible.

But the doctor is right, and she knows it. She attended an American Heart Association event a few weeks ago and completed the speaker's quiz to figure out her risk of heart disease. Crossing out all the circles was kind of scary: her dad had a heart attack at 57.

Charlene's cholesterol is a little high, and truth be told, she isn't getting much exercise because she spends so much time in the car. As a result, she's carrying extra weight. Writing an "S" in 40 circles because her stress is so high was a wakeup call. The day after the event, she made an appointment to discuss her risk factors with her doctor. She knows something has to change.

Example Stress Burden Assessment Worksheet – Charleen's Results

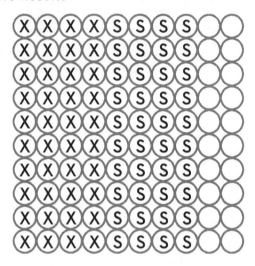

While Charlene's results may seem extreme, they really aren't unusual. Unless you know the problem and how big the problem is, it is very hard to solve it. Most of us don't have tools to measure the physical impact of stress. Defining a problem is the best first step to solving it. This assessment offers that.

Use the worksheet on the next page with the assessment questions in Chapter 3.

Your Stress Burden Assessment Worksheet

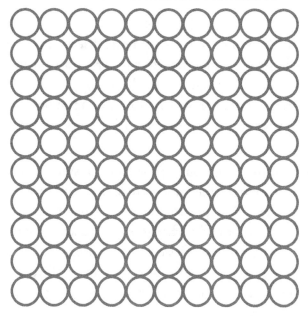

I've watched many people struggle with marking an "S" in their circles because they are shocked by the impact of their stress. But it is important to be honest with yourself about your health.

How many of your circles have an "S" in them? This is the impact stress is placing on your physical health. Stress presses the fast-forward button on heart disease.

For example, if you have ten circles marked with an "S," you may develop heart disease ten years earlier. How much time and quality of life is stress taking away from you?

So, now what?

As you work to limit your risk of heart disease and stress-proof your heart, it is important to partner with your health provider to take advantage of all the tools available. Like Charlene, the first step should be to make an appointment with your doctor to discuss all your risk factors and how to manage them.

While we can't change our age or family history, there are many ways to control other risk factors. Too often we avoid going to the doctor to prevent ourselves from hearing bad news. The truth is, our bodies change over time, and with those changes our risk factors can tick slowly higher. Regular checkups and candid conversations with your doctor about all your risk factors can nip a problem in the bud instead of having to treat a life-threatening problem later.

Cortisol isn't the enemy

Jesse is an ER nurse in a busy metropolitan-area hospital. Near the end of a 12-hour shift, Jesse is tired, but he scrambles to meet the ambulances bringing patients from a multiple-car accident. Suddenly, he's not tired. With speed and skill, he meets the gurneys, triaging and directing staff. In less than an hour, all the patients are stabilized and receiving treatment.

Jesse stands at the nurses' station, shakes out his arms, and takes a few deep breaths. He feels the tingly energy of the emergency draining from his body. He performed well, and he feels a sense of calm as he heads home. His hardwired cortisol reaction to the incoming patients made it possible for him to do his job, even though he was tired. The sense of "ahhhh" after the crisis passed is the sign that his cortisol level is falling back to normal.

Life without the zing of excitement of cortisol would be boring. Stress-proof people use the cortisol reaction to respond to stressors (both good and bad) and then efficiently process it out of their bodies. If we can bring the cortisol levels back to normal and keep them there most of the time, we can reduce the risk of heart disease down to the things we can't change, such as age and ethnicity.

Fortunately, your body is designed to process cortisol, if you let it.

Activities that direct your body to reduce cortisol and help process it out of your system offset the physical impact of your stress.

Ordinary activities, such as standing up and taking a quick walk once per hour, can significantly lower your cortisol level. Not only is this type of activity good for your heart, but it also has added benefits such as increased attention, fewer muscle aches from extended sitting, and better blood flow to the brain, which supports creativity and critical thought.

Use the zing of cortisol to get that project completed or assist your client in a time of need, and then use the five strategies in Section 2 to help your body efficiently eliminate cortisol.

We all need to keep cortisol levels low to protect our hearts. If your risk is high, controlling cortisol levels is critical. For me, with my heart history, the strategies in Section 2 are essential skills to keep my heart strong.

A stress-proof heart is strong enough to power a fulfilling life and resilient enough to withstand high stress, change, crisis, and to bounce back from illness.

Is it time to call 911?

One of my most popular YouTube videos answers the question "Is it time to call 911?" So many people wait too long to seek help when they are having a heart attack. The sooner you get help, the better the outcome will be. Don't drive yourself to the hospital. Calling 911 means you will start receiving life-saving treatment as soon as the first responders arrive.

Do you have:

- Unusual pain in your back, abdomen, shoulder, neck, chest, or jaw?
- Shortness of breath or trouble breathing (especially while sleeping or lying down)?
- Cold sweat?
- Racing heartbeat or the feeling of fluttering or missed beats?
- Pressure in your chest?
- Lightheadedness?

💜 Unusual and unexplained vomiting?

If you answered yes to ANY of these symptoms, it is time to call 911. These are signs you may be having a heart attack.

What does a heart attack feel like?

My heart attack started out feeling like heartburn. I was seven months pregnant with twins, so heartburn wasn't unusual. But very quickly things changed. I started vomiting, and my chest felt like my bra was five sizes too small. What at first seemed to be heartburn quickly became so intense that I knew I was in trouble.

We all know what is normal for our bodies. Paying attention to unusual symptoms could mean the difference between life and death. This is especially important for women. Women's heart attack symptoms are often subtle and difficult to diagnose, even for professionals.

So, is that sharp, burning sensation in your chest caused by the pizza you just ate or a sign of something more serious?

Here are some ways to tell the difference:

💜 Did exercise or physical activity bring on the symptoms? If it did, this is a big clue to get help right away. It is time to call 911.

💜 Is the pain stopping you from doing normal activities? Heartburn can be uncomfortable, but pain that distracts you from work or causes you to withdraw from activities should be evaluated by a medical professional quickly. It is time to call 911.

♥ Do you have risk factors for heart attack? High blood pressure, high cholesterol, high stress, being overweight, being sedentary, and having family members with heart disease are signs you may be more likely to be having a heart attack. It is time to call 911.

♥ Did you just eat something that upset your stomach? If your tummy is usually upset 30 to 40 minutes after eating spicy or greasy food, the chances are it is heartburn. But if you haven't eaten, or if what you ate doesn't usually cause stomach upset, then it is cause for concern. It is time to call 911.

♥ Does an antacid help? Usually the relief is immediate. If you take an H2 blocker such as Zantac or Tagamet, relief should come in 30 to 40 minutes. If the pain continues or gets worse, seek medical attention right away. It is time to call 911.

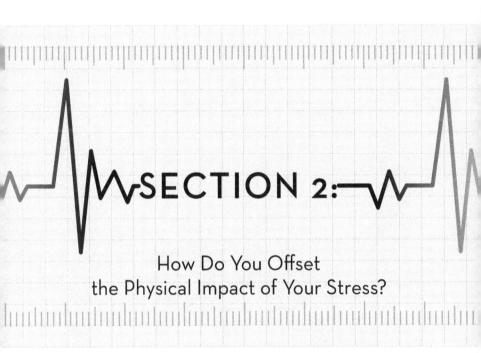

SECTION 2:

How Do You Offset the Physical Impact of Your Stress?

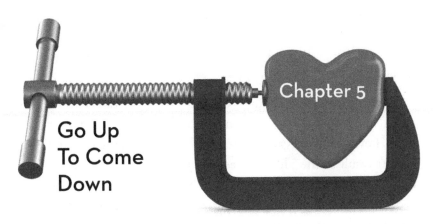

Chapter 5

Go Up
To Come
Down

There are two minutes left in the playoff game. If the team makes the field goal, they are going to the Super Bowl! Decked out for the home team, Jerome, Patricia, and Steve have been on their feet, cheering at the television throughout the hard-fought game. Jerry can feel his heart racing as the kicker lines up. Patricia is peeking through her fingers, hardly able to watch—the pressure is intense. Steve is rocking back and forth in his seat, willing the ball to go through the goalposts.

It does!

After high fives and cheering, all three fall back into their seats. Jerome takes a deep breath and is amazed by how great he feels. His pulse comes down, and his body settles.

That "ahhhh" feeling of your heart rate coming down is an indication that your cortisol level is coming down too.

Any activity that raises your heart rate for a few minutes and then allows it to come back down can help reduce your cortisol level. So, could watching an exciting game actually reduce your stress? That may depend on who wins, but our emotions can undoubtedly raise our heart rate.

If at the end of the game, you feel your heart rate settling down, know that cortisol is coming down as well. This doesn't work, however, if the game or activity leaves you amped up and doesn't result in the "ahhhhh" feeling of your heart rate coming down. Harnessing the connection between heart rate and cortisol levels is a very effective way to process cortisol and offset the physical impact of stress.

Exercise as the antidote for stress

Exercise conditions the heart and makes it work more efficiently. It lowers blood pressure and blood sugar. It clears bad cholesterol from your body and limits the number of triglycerides formed by converting the calories you eat into energy. It also releases hormones that reduce pain and calm the brain. Exercise also helps purge your body of cortisol.

Engaging in aerobic exercise, which elevates and sustains the heart rate at 55 to 85 percent of your maximum heart rate for 20 to 30 minutes, several times per week can cut your risk of heart disease in half. For most of us, a brisk walk is enough to raise our heart rates into the aerobic zone.

Exercise's powerful combination of physical benefits and reduction of cortisol makes it a crucial method of stress-proofing your heart. It both lessens your risk of heart disease and limits the adverse effects of cortisol. Not only will you feel better when you exercise, but the reduction of the cortisol in your system will help your brain work more effectively, too.

Nearly everyone gets some amount of activity during the day. The goal is to increase the amount of time you are moving. An obvious way to move more is to carve out 20 to 30 minutes of the day to walk, ride a bike, or do some other traditional cardiovascular exercise. This may work on some days but be difficult on others.

Luckily it is not the only answer.

How do you fit more physical activity into your day?

If you can get to the gym or do traditional exercise a few days a week, great! What do you do on the other days or as an alternative? You can efficiently process cortisol with a combination of conventional exercise on some days, everyday activities, and other ideas in this chapter.

Use everyday activities:

Any activity that increases your heart rate, quickens your breath, and gives you a little "glow" counts as moderately intense cardiovascular activity.

Think about a 30-minute walk as the basis for comparison. Some household chores such as raking, mowing the lawn, or using a snowblower are equivalent in intensity. So, in other words, 30 minutes spent mowing the lawn (with a push mower, not a riding mower) is the same as taking a 30-minute walk.

Running is a more intense activity and will give you the same cardiovascular benefit in 15 minutes. Shoveling snow and hauling landscaping materials is more intense, as well. Walking is still good for you, but it will take 60 minutes to receive the same benefit. Doing less intense chores such as gardening, painting, and cleaning are also helpful ways to stay active.

Everyday activities are a great way to meet your daily physical activity goal. Targeting activities in your day can fulfill your commitment when there isn't time for more traditional exercise.

The table on pages 60-61 gives examples of a variety of activities at different levels of intensity to help you choose. Balancing the intensity of your activity with the time in your schedule can help you meet your goal of improving your heart health and reducing your cortisol level.

A word of warning: Starting with a more intense activity can lead to symptoms such as lightheadedness, nausea, and even chest pain. Oftentimes, when people set a new exercise goal, they don't pay attention to their bodies and work out too intensely. It is a good idea to have a conversation with your doctor or a trainer about what level of intensity is right for you. When in doubt, start with a less intense activity. Also, keep in mind that jumping right into a high-intensity activity can cause injury. Allow your body to warm up.

Use chunks of activities:

Breaking your activity into 10- or 15-minute chunks may be more convenient on busy days. Try these ideas to take your heart rate and cortisol up and down:

💜 Taking the dog for a 15-minute walk twice per day can fulfill your body's need for physical activity.

💜 Park farther away or take a lap around your building before you start work.

💜 Walk the halls at break time or at lunch. (However, you must keep going. Encourage those who want to chat to walk with you!)

💜 When traveling, plan to walk 15 minutes between security and your gate, and between the plane and baggage claim—you'll be good for the day.

Make the most of being on your feet:

Strap on a pedometer and count your steps (10,000 steps is equivalent to a 30-minute brisk walk). Any time you can make the pedometer click, you've done the equivalent of a step. Make the most of being on your feet by:

💜 Wiggling your hips while standing in line or brushing your teeth

💜 Pacing while talking on the phone

Physical Activity Table

Intensity	Time	Walking/ Running	Sports
Low	60 minutes	2 miles @ 2 mph	golf, badminton, croquet, bowling, shuffleboard, table tennis, and softball
Moderate/ Low	45 minutes	1.75 miles @ 3 mph	volleyball, touch football, roller blading, rock climbing, & ice skating
Baseline Moderate	30 minutes	2 miles @ 4 mph Pushing stroller 1.5 miles@ 3 mph	doubles tennis, gymnastics, baseball, hockey, basketball, soccer, & cross country skiing
Moderate/High	20 minutes	1.5 miles @ 4.5 mph (run or fast walk)	lap swimming, singles tennis, & racquetball
High	15 minutes	1.5 miles @ 6 mph (run) Stair climbing	singles tennis, bicycling 16 mph

Chores	"Gym" Activities	Seated Activities	"Fun" Activities
washing/waxing car, ironing, folding laundry, washing dishes	yoga, pilates, tae kwon do, free weights or machines	arm raises & circles, any household chores	frisbee, catch, batting practice
yard work (fertilizing, seeding, hand digging), cleaning house, woodworking, & painting walls	cardio w/ weights, resistance bands or balance ball	wheeling in wheelchair, arm excercises w/ weights/ bands	play in the pool, play in the snow
raking, sweeping, using push lawn mower or snowblower	water aerobics, cardio, dance (tap, ballet, ballroom) cardio, circuit, martial arts, Zumba	dynamic seated aerobics, fast wheeling in wheelchair	shooting baskets, kicking soccer ball, social dancing, tag, & bike riding (10-14 mph)
shoveling snow & digging holes	ski machine, elliptical, rowing machine	wheel chair basketball or rugby	
hauling rocks or other heavy items, & chopping down trees	jumping rope, high impact aerobics, spinning class, & step class		

What works for you?

Think about ideas for working more ways to "Go Up to Come Down" into your day. Use the following prompts to write down some activities you can use:

What low-intensity activity could you do at the end of the day to help lower your cortisol level before bedtime (a walk around the neighborhood, tidying up around your home, or yoga, for example)?

_____

_____

_____

_____

_____

What "screen time" activities are highly engaging and raise your heart rate (sports, suspenseful television programs, or interactive video games, for example)?

_____

_____

_____

_____

_____

Which moderate to high-intensity activities do you enjoy? Which one(s) could you work into your day more often?

_____

_____

_____

_____

_____

When can you fit in a few extra steps or a little bit of activity?

_____

_____

_____

_____

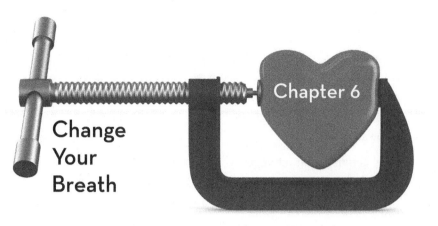

Change
Your
Breath

S tuck in traffic once again, Chantel feels her pulse rising. Remembering a tip from an employee wellness event, she flips on the radio and pulls up her "stuck in traffic" playlist on her phone. As Beyoncé starts singing about "All the Single Ladies," Chantel sings along at the top of her lungs. Not only is being stuck in traffic a bit more enjoyable with a soundtrack, but Chantel feels calmer and more energized as she finally pulls into the parking lot.

When we are stressed, we take short, shallow breaths. Slowing down your breathing directs your body to lower cortisol levels. Changing the pattern of your breath feels good too. Singing is a great way to change the length and depth of breath and has been shown to act as a natural antidepressant. Most people feel calmer and more energized after singing. This means that blasting your favorite song and singing along while stuck in traffic is a great stress-reduction strategy!

Laughter works the same way. When we laugh, we disrupt our breathing pattern and release endorphins into the system, just like singing. Watching a funny movie, talking with a witty friend, or surfing silly videos on your phone can be great ways to elevate your mood and reduce cortisol by changing your breath. (Do yourself a favor and google "Pancakey Wife Video"—you won't be sorry.)

Any activity that changes your breathing pattern works. This is why meditation and yoga are often suggested for stress reduction. More aerobic activities change your breath, too.

At an event for human resources professionals, an audience member shared a strategy to transition from work mode to home mode and back again. She has specific "walk-in" songs programmed. Singing along to the songs not only puts her in the right frame of mind, but it also sends her in calm and energized. Great idea!

Use the prompts below to identify opportunities to change your breath:

In the morning, when do you feel your breath shortening or your pulse rising?

_____

_____

How can you change your breath during those times?

_____

_____

During the workday, are there regular times you feel your breath shortening or your pulse rising?

_____

_____

_____

_____

How can you change your breath during those times?

_____

_____

_____

_____

When are your times of transition?

_____

_____

_____

_____

How can you change your breath during those times?

_____

_____

_____

_____

In the evening, when do you feel your breath shortening or your pulse rising?

_____

_____

_____

_____

How can you change your breath during those times?

_____

_____

_____

_____

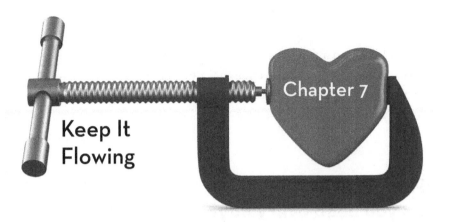

Keep It Flowing

Chapter 7

T he plane was hot and smelly. They'd been sitting on the tarmac for more than an hour, and Patricia wasn't feeling well. She shifted in her seat and pulled at her top and waistband, which all felt too tight. Taking her water bottle out of her bag, Patricia was frustrated to find it empty. She didn't have a chance to fill it this morning when she flew in for the meeting at the regional office. This had been a packed day with few breaks. There was barely time for lunch, and she didn't drink much during the day, either.

She took some deep breaths and tried to calm down. Why was her heart beating so fast? Suddenly, she felt like her heart was a fish flopping around in her chest. The woman in the seat next to her asked if Patricia was okay. Patricia just shook her head, and the kind stranger pushed the button to get the flight attendant's attention.

It turns out, Patricia was experiencing atrial fibrillation, the most common type of abnormal heart rhythm.

Patricia's story is an extreme example of the danger of dehydration. As one of my dietitian friends likes to say, "You can't float a log down a dry stream." One of the biggest favors you can do for your body is to drink enough water. Staying hydrated also protects your heart and stops the stress of your body's reaction to dehydration from triggering a cortisol response.

How much water do you need every day?

Your body needs water to regulate temperature, digest food, eliminate waste, and keep your blood flowing. If your body doesn't get enough water, it will hold on to fat, and your blood will thicken. If you have reached a plateau in weight loss or have trouble managing your blood pressure, pay attention to the amount of water you drink each day.

The bigger the body—the more fluid you need. Without the proper amount of water, your body doesn't function correctly. It is more than just dry skin or dry mouth—dehydration reduces your body's ability to flow. This can result in achy joints and muscles, high blood pressure, reduced kidney function, and that's just the start of the list of possible issues.

A good rule of thumb to determine the minimum amount of water you should drink each day is to divide your weight (in pounds) by two. You should drink at least that number of ounces of water each day.

For example:

Weight: 150 lbs.

$150 \div 2 = 75$

This person should drink 75 ounces of water per day. Consult your doctor or Registered Dietitian Nutritionist to figure out how much water you need to drink based on your health needs, exercise load, and climate.

Does it have to be water?

Well, no, but water is best for the majority of your fluid intake. Water doesn't contain anything more—no calories, no additives, nothing extra; it is just water.

If you don't like drinking plain water, you can dress it up with:

💜 Unsweetened herbal tea (hot or cold)

💜 A squirt of fruit juice

💜 Bubbles (carbonated water)

Other beverages can be used in moderation to fulfill your need for fluid:

💜 Unsweetened coffee is fine as some of your fluids, although it contains caffeine, but no additional calories. Limit it to three or four cups per day. Some people shouldn't drink caffeine at all. Talk to your doctor about how much caffeine per day is healthy for you.

♥ Milk works well for some of your fluid intake. The added calories are offset by the beneficial vitamins and minerals.

♥ Fruit juices carry quite a few calories and should be watered down or limited to a small glass per day.

Things you shouldn't count in your daily fluid intake:

♥ Soda: Treat soda as liquid candy—it is loaded with calories your body doesn't need and often can't use.

♥ Diet soda: High levels of sodium may counteract your hydration efforts.

♥ Sports drinks: Unless you need to replace electrolytes because you have been profusely sweating for an extended period of time, you should not use a sports drink in lieu of water. Originally designed to aid athletes losing electrolytes through sweat, sports drinks have somehow become a casual beverage. Seriously, it isn't a "health drink"—stop it.

How Does Plane Travel Trigger Heart Problems?

According to Mellanie True Hills, CEO of StopAfib. org, a patient advocacy organization that hosts the number-one arrhythmia site and one of the top five heart disease sites worldwide, "The significantly dry air on a plane wicks moisture out of the body, causing dehydration quickly. Dehydration thickens the blood and can deplete the body of essential minerals such as potassium and magnesium. Magnesium regulates the heart rhythm and potassium helps it work. Inadequate levels of potassium or magnesium can trigger abnormal heart rhythms, including atrial fibrillation (afib)."

She continues: "If your heart has ever felt like a flopping fish, a bag of wiggly worms, or fluttering butterflies, you may have atrial fibrillation, the most common irregular heartbeat."

For some people, afib symptoms are fleeting and disappear on their own. However, the abnormal rhythm can cause blood not to be pushed out of the heart to the rest of the body, and thus it pools and can form a clot. Already-thickened blood from dehydration makes this more likely. That clot could then travel to the brain and cause a stroke.

Afib is just one of many types of abnormal heart rhythms that can make up holiday heart syndrome, a condition whose name derives from emergency rooms seeing an increase of people with heart trouble during holidays such as Christmas, New Year's Day, spring break, and Super Bowl Sunday. Overindulgence in food and alcohol causes an abnormal heart rhythm and chest pain. Business travelers, especially those going to conferences, often have the same overindulgence issues. Adding dehydration to the mix can trigger chest pain, palpitations, or shortness of breath, which should not be ignored.

"Drinking mineral water, or even club soda, not only helps keep you hydrated but also helps replace the minerals you are losing. I think jet lag is mostly caused by dehydration, and by drinking mineral water both during the trip and when I arrive, I rarely suffer from it even when traveling internationally," suggests Mellanie. She recommends drinking at least six to twelve ounces of water per hour on the plane. Yes, this means you will have to get up and use the restroom, which in itself is an excellent way to avoid a blood clot.

Are you getting enough water each day?

Keep track today and find out. Experiment with increasing your intake. How does it make you feel? Yes, you may have to visit the restroom more often, but a bit more walking doesn't hurt either!

Drink up!

Use the prompts below to identify opportunities to increase your water intake:

How much water do you need each day?

Your weight (in pounds):

_____

Divide your weight by 2 to find:

Number of ounces of water per day:

_____

Thinking about your water intake in four time periods of the day can help you get enough.

Divide your number of ounces needed per day by 4 to find:

Number of ounces per time period:

_____

First Time Period: Start of day

How much water (or other beverages) do you drink before you start work?

_____ ounces

Is this more or less than that the amount you need for each time period? How many more ounces should you be drinking?

_____ ounces

Second Time Period: First three hours of work

How much water (or other beverages) do you drink in the first three hours of work?

_____ ounces

Is this more or less than that the amount you need for each time period? How many more ounces should you be drinking?

_____ ounces

Third Time Period: Second three hours of work

How much water (or other beverages) do you drink in the second three hours of work?

_____ ounces

Is this more or less than that the amount you need for each time period? How many more ounces should you be drinking?

_____ ounces

Fourth Time Period: Transition from work to home

How much water (or other beverages) do you drink in the last hours of work and the first hour at home? (Keep in mind that many people need to limit fluid intake in the four hours before bedtime to sleep through the night.)

_____ ounces

Is this more or less than that the amount you need for each time period? How many more ounces should you be drinking?

_____ ounces

Keep It Fueled

Steve isn't a big fan of vegetables; he'd rather grab a hamburger and fries at lunch. But after his last checkup, he knows some things have to change. He remembers a tip from an employee wellness webinar last week and looks at the menu for something colorful. There is a quinoa bowl with vegetables and chicken. That sounds colorful. As it turns out, it is pretty tasty, too.

Eating well provides the fuel to run your body and brain. Hunger increases stress and cortisol levels. Fueling your body doesn't have to be complicated. Ignore fad diets, celebrity lifestyles, and television doctors, and stick to a few simple strategies.

Your body needs protein, water, carbohydrates, and fat to function correctly. It uses what it needs for power and stores the rest as fat for later use. The trick is figuring out what to feed your body to fuel it well and not leave too much behind. Eating better doesn't require you to turn down everything you enjoy, but rather to make good choices and seek out foods that will give you the fuel and energy to make it to the next snack or meal.

Eat fruits and vegetables

The Center for Disease Control says only one out of ten adults eats enough fruits and vegetables. I'm not suggesting that everyone become a vegetarian; however, we need to do better. The average adult should have at least five servings of fruits and veggies every day.

We can get caught up in marketing around the "right" kinds of fruits and vegetables to choose. Keep it simple.

I don't care if you choose the store-brand carrot or the locally sourced, organic one. Just eat a carrot!

Here are some ideas to get more fruits and veggies:

- For breakfast, blend up a smoothie. Choose whole grain toast with peanut butter and banana slices or old-fashioned oatmeal with raisins and nuts.

- At lunch, choose something with lots of colors, such as a salad, stir-fry, or soup, rather than something brown or beige (e.g., hamburger and French fries).

- During dinner, limit your portion of lean protein to about the size of a deck of cards and then fill the rest of your plate with vegetables and fruits.

- When snacking, grab a handful of trail mix with nuts and dried fruit. Try baby carrots and hummus or a good old-fashioned apple.

For additional tips on how to get more fruits and vegetables, recipes, and information on eating better, visit the Academy of Nutrition and Dietetics website: EatRight.org.

Enjoy treats

All food fits in a healthy diet and too much of anything can be unhealthy. The goal is to enjoy a variety of food in moderation, even food containing sugar, fat, salt or any other "bad" ingredients. Denying yourself the food you love—for example, chocolate— can derail good intentions because we can become focused on what we "can't" have, or eat too much of other foods to compensate for feeling deprived. Have a treat every once in a while. Choose something indulgent and savor it.

Ask a real expert

If you wonder about the right combination of foods you should be eating, don't rely on a nutritionist at the gym, a spa, or someone trying to sell a product. Instead, rely on a Registered Dietitian Nutritionist (RDN). RDNs are the experts on nutrition and have the latest scientifically-based information on healthy eating. Find one at EatRight.org/find-an-expert.

Pay attention to how you feel

Your body has unique needs for fuel. Do you feel better eating three small meals per day and a couple of snacks? Skipping breakfast will slow your metabolism and make it more difficult for your body to use the food you finally give it later in the day. As you experiment with adding more fruits and vegetables to your diet, notice how much protein and complex carbohydrates (whole grains, for example) you need to combine with them to keep your energy up and your hunger at bay until the next meal or snack.

Use the prompts below to identify opportunities to keep your body fueled:

What did you eat this morning?

_____

_____

_____

How did you feel after you ate? Did you feel fueled for your activities?

_____

_____

_____

Did you have a mid-morning snack? What did you eat?

_____

_____

_____

How did you feel after you ate? Did you feel fueled for your activities?

_____

_____

_____

Did you eat lunch? What did you have?

_____

_____

_____

How did you feel after you ate? Did you feel fueled for your activities?

_____

_____

_____

Did you have a mid-afternoon snack? What did you eat?

_____

_____

_____

How did you feel after you ate? Did you feel fueled for your activities?

_____

_____

_____

Did you eat dinner? What did you have?

_____

_____

_____

How did you feel after you ate? Did you feel fueled for your activities?

_____

_____

_____

Did you have a snack before bed? What did you eat?

_____

_____

_____

How did you feel after you ate? Did you sleep well?

_____

_____

_____

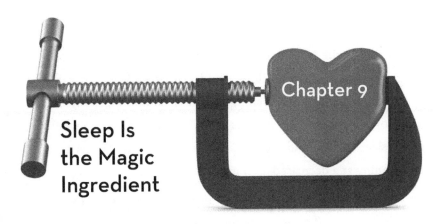

Sleep Is the Magic Ingredient

Chapter 9

Charlene unpacked her "sleep kit" again. After three nights in three different hotels, she was ready to go home. Travel is just part of her job managing her sales team. She used to think she could catch up on sleep when she got back home, but it never really seemed to work. Her doctor told her sleep was the most important thing she could do to reduce her cortisol level. So, she put together a kit of things to help her sleep on the road. She has a sleep mask and a noise machine. Her son searched online and found a small folding fan to keep her cool. Her doctor suggested an herbal supplement to help her doze off. As silly as it seems, she packed a pillow, too—one that smells like home.

As I tell my audiences, "Sleep is the magic ingredient that makes everything else work." You can exercise, eat right, and do everything your doctor says you should, but without enough good-quality, consistent sleep, it won't work.

Poor sleep is also associated with anxiety and depression. Even more concerning, a recent lab-based research study conducted by the National Institutes of Health tied the lack of sleep with severe cognitive decreases. In fact, they found that if, over two weeks, you are sleeping less than six hours per night, your cognitive and reflex abilities are the same as someone who didn't sleep for two full nights. This means that most of us are functioning at a decreased level most of the time!

Sleep is essential to a stress-proof heart for two reasons. First, sleep is the most efficient way to purge cortisol from your system. Second, lack of sleep can cause the buildup of plaque.

Why is plaque terrible for your heart and brain?

Think of plaque as sludge forming on the inside of pipes. As plaque builds, the artery walls thicken, which narrows the space available for blood to flow. Ultimately, the buildup of plaque slows down the flow of blood. This reduced blood flow robs cells of the oxygen they need. This type of heart disease, atherosclerosis, is often referred to as "hardening of the arteries."

- When these plaque deposits are in arteries that supply the heart, it is called coronary artery disease, and it can cause a heart attack.

- When they form in the arteries that supply the arms and legs, it is called peripheral artery disease.

♥ When they form in the arteries that supply the brain, it can cause a stroke and is associated with Alzheimer's and dementia.

How much sleep do you need?

Six hours seems to be the bare minimum per night. Seven or eight is better, and more than nine appears to be too much.

Along with damaging your heart, lack of sleep can rob you of efficiency and make any task harder. Your body will eventually force you to sleep. If you need a cup of coffee to keep going or find yourself dozing at your desk, it likely isn't because your job is boring—you are tired!

Are you getting enough sleep?

Check the box if you experience the following:

☐ Do you find your mind wandering when reading a magazine article?

☐ Do you have trouble focusing your eyes when you are driving?

☐ Do you hit the snooze button several times each morning?

☐ Do you feel like the volume is turned up on your emotions?

☐ Do you forget appointments or important dates?

☐ Do you carry extra weight around your middle, no matter how much you count calories or exercise?

☐ Do you doze off while working on the computer or watching television?

If you answer yes to any of the questions, you may not be getting enough sleep. If you are getting the sleep you need, you will wake up—without an alarm—feeling rested, refreshed, and ready to meet the day.

Tips for a better night's sleep:

❤ Limit caffeine past the early afternoon.

❤ Avoid using alcohol to induce sleep, as it causes interrupted and restless sleep.

❤ Be active for at least 30 minutes per day.

❤ Create a quiet, dark, and cool space to sleep.

❤ Turn off devices and avoid blue light screens as you wind down for bed.

❤ Pay attention to your bed, linens, and pillow. Small adjustments can increase comfort and bring better sleep.

❤ Talk with your doctor about any health conditions that may make sleep more elusive.

Also, discuss any herbal or medical remedies that may ease chronic sleeplessness.

Even if you try all of those tips, the stress chemical, cortisol, can make it difficult to fall asleep. One of the best things you can do to get more sleep is to disconnect from stress triggers in the two to three hours before bed.

Because I feel strongly about giving you enough information to make a difference in your health, I'm including a bonus chapter with insights on strategies to disengage from emotional stress to allow your cortisol level to come down. This chapter is from *Stress-Proof Your Life*, a book about becoming immune to unavoidable stress. Please also check out the sneak peek of *Stress-Proof Your Life* at the end of this book.

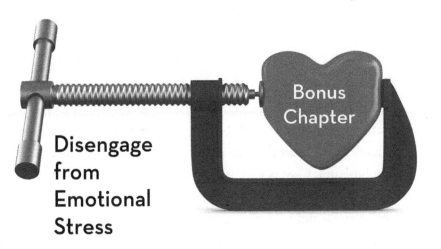

Disengage from Emotional Stress

A ll of the strategies in *Stress-Proof Your Heart* work only if cortisol has stopped pumping into the system. Emotional stress reactions, however, continue to pump cortisol into the body even when the stressor isn't present. This is why stress can keep us up at night. High cortisol levels make it hard to sleep, which leads to thinking about stressful things, which then pumps even more cortisol into the system. It can be a vicious cycle.

Your body needs to be able to recover from emotional stress, and this is where I think most stress-management programs fail. Stress recovery is not a one-size-fits-all proposition.

Most stress-reduction strategies tend toward the quiet, contemplative activities. These activities work well for some people, but for others, sitting quietly and concentrating on their breathing increases their stress because they can't shut off thinking about the things causing them stress. We all have different needs for distraction, contemplation, engagement, and solitude when it comes to stress recovery.

This was comically demonstrated while on vacation in Mexico celebrating my husband's 50th birthday. We traveled with five other adults to a resort that caters to scuba divers. I don't dive, but my husband, Clay, is enthusiastic about the sport, as were our fellow travelers. This interaction led to some fascinating insight on stress and relaxation.

When not diving, most of our group spent time lounging by the pool, with the iguanas (yes, actual iguanas). Being fair-skinned, I spent some enjoyable time by the pool, in the shade, reading. Clay did not, however, have the staying power of the rest of the group. He enjoyed being an iguana for a while, but then also needed to DO something. We took out the little sailboat, went for walks—coming and going from the pool.

One of our fellow travelers remarked to Clay, "You are always on the go. When are you going to relax?"

Here's the thing—he was relaxing.

Clay joked at dinner one evening, "I'm like a border collie: if I don't have something to do, I start chewing on things."

This is both funny and true. It is also a great description of how he relaxes. He needs something diverting him from thinking about the things that cause stress. Staying still provides him with too much time to think. Our vacations tend to be action-packed, but we've come to recognize that I need some "iguana time" along the way to get what I need to disengage and recover from stress.

How do you disengage?

Too often we think of relaxation in only one facet: stillness. Meditation works for many "iguanas," but if you are a border collie at heart, it may cause more stress to try to be still.

Hobbies are excellent for reducing stress. My dad, for example, loved woodworking and spent hours in his garage workshop building, sanding, and finishing. The "busy hands/free mind" essence of these actions can reduce stress for many people.

Other people need physical activities to reduce stress. Racing on an all-women sailing crew last summer, I saw this in action. All of us have demanding jobs, but running from one side of the boat to the other, working as a team to deploy sails and build speed, as well laughing when things didn't go as planned, reduced our stress because we were entirely focused on the task at hand.

Your way of relaxing might not look the same as it does for your spouse, co-worker, or friend, but that is okay. Embrace your own style and make time for activities to support your stress reduction. People often fall somewhere in the middle between border collie and iguana. The trick is to give yourself permission to make the time for activities that will allow you to disengage and recover from emotional stress.

Are you an iguana or a border collie?

Understanding and embracing the type of activities you need to disengage from stress—your Stress Recovery Personality—is essential to stress-proofing your heart.

The following quiz will help you determine if you are an iguana or a border collie. Use the answer sheet on below to mark your answer, or take the quiz online at StressProofBook.com.

Stress Recovery Personality Quiz

Check the answer to each question:

1.	☐	A	☐	B	☐	C	☐	D	☐ E
2.	☐	A	☐	B	☐	C	☐	D	☐ E
3.	☐	A	☐	B	☐	C	☐	D	☐ E
4.	☐	A	☐	B	☐	C	☐	D	☐ E
5.	☐	A	☐	B	☐	C	☐	D	☐ E

1. Imagine it is a Tuesday night. You miraculously have left work at 5:30 and have two hours of free time. If you have children, Mary Poppins is in town and will put them to bed. You don't have to finish any work, and you don't have to make dinner for anyone if you don't want to. How would you like to spend that time?

   Would you like to:

   A. Sleep?

   B. Watch your guilty-pleasure television program?

   C. Cook dinner and have a glass of wine with your partner?

   D. Do a project around the house, tidy up, or organize something?

   E. Go to the gym and get your sweat on?

2. It is Friday night and—again—if you have children, Mary Poppins has taken them to her house for a sleepover. How would you like to spend that time?

   Would you like to:

   A. Binge-watch something?

   B. Go to a bookstore, art supply shop, or other "poke-around" location?

   C. Attend a play or movie?

   D. Have dinner out with friends?

   E. Go somewhere with music, friends, and dancing?

3. It is Saturday afternoon, and it is a beautiful day. How would you like to spend that time?

   Does your day include:

   A. A hammock, a book, and a refreshing beverage?

   B. A computer, Wi-Fi, and coffee?

   C. Paints, crafts, or carpentry?

   D. Dirt, plants, and a little sweat?

   E. Sneakers, athletic clothing, and maybe a little competition?

4. It is late Sunday morning and another beautiful day. Where would you spend the next few hours?

   Are you:

   A. Still in bed sleeping?

   B. Doing the Sunday crossword puzzle?

   C. Out for brunch?

   D. In the park with friends or your dog?

   E. Out biking or exploring?

5. On vacation, what type of activity would you most enjoy?

   Would you:

   A. Find a quiet spot to read, rest, and recover?

   B. Use a guide to find the best places for local food?

   C. Take a walking tour of a new town?

D. Hike to a secluded waterfall?

E. Zip-line in a remote area?

Understanding Your Stress Recovery Personality Quiz Results

Your Stress Recovery Personality indicates the type of activity most likely to lower your cortisol level by allowing you to disengage from the source of stress. Some people need highly engaging activities, while others benefit from being more contemplative.

Where are most of your marks on your Stress Recovery Personality Quiz Results?

1. ☐ A	☐ B	☐ C	☐ D	☐ E
2. ☐ A	☐ B	☐ C	☐ D	☐ E
3. ☐ A	☐ B	☐ C	☐ D	☐ E
4. ☐ A	☐ B	☐ C	☐ D	☐ E
5. ☐ A	☐ B	☐ C	☐ D	☐ E

A. If most of your answers are A, you are an iguana. As an iguana, the most effective stress recovery activities are contemplative and allow you to be calm and recover from things causing you stress. Try activities such as:

- meditating
- quiet walks in nature
- drawing
- watercolor painting
- model building
- photography
- puzzles
- genealogy
- chess
- reading
- singing/playing music for your own enjoyment
- collecting stamps or coins
- astronomy
- knitting
- sewing
- crochet
- quilting
- jewelry making
- floral arranging
- astronomy

- ♥ watching television
- ♥ scrapbooking
- ♥ visiting museums

B. If your answers are clustered toward the left (mostly Bs and Cs) you are an iguana with border collie tendencies. The most effective stress recovery activities will occupy the brain and allow you to create calm and recover from things causing you stress. Try activities such as:

- ♥ woodworking
- ♥ car restoration
- ♥ archery
- ♥ pool/billiards
- ♥ cooking
- ♥ baking
- ♥ learning a new language
- ♥ card playing
- ♥ home brewing/winemaking
- ♥ computer programming
- ♥ gaming
- ♥ bird watching
- ♥ yoga
- ♥ storytelling
- ♥ shopping

- ❤ antiquing
- ❤ binge-watching television
- ❤ social media
- ❤ going to the movies
- ❤ going to the theater
- ❤ going out with friends
- ❤ trivia contests
- ❤ ballroom dancing
- ❤ gardening
- ❤ camping
- ❤ fishing
- ❤ bowling
- ❤ magic
- ❤ writing/blogging
- ❤ volunteering
- ❤ singing/playing with other people
- ❤ metal detecting
- ❤ beekeeping
- ❤ meteorology
- ❤ caring for animals
- ❤ board games
- ❤ a book club
- ❤ travel by train or car

- kite flying
- biking
- golf
- visiting zoos
- sport coaching or officiating
- fantasy sports
- wine tasting
- cooking classes
- weight lifting
- watching sports with friends
- service groups or clubs
- listening to music
- going to shows—auto, home and garden, boat, sports, etc.

C. If your answers are mostly Cs, you aren't alone! Many of us shift between iguana and border collie depending on the situation. In some moments you may choose a calm, contemplative activity, and in others an active, engaging activity will serve you better. Choose activities from the other lists to fit your needs.

D. If your answers are clustered toward the right (mostly Cs and Ds), you are a border collie with iguana tendencies. The most effective stress recovery activities are highly engaging and allow you to be distracted from things causing you stress. Try activities such as:

- geocaching
- running
- martial arts
- hiking
- sailing
- kayaking
- canoeing
- hunting
- backpacking
- dance class
- swimming
- improv
- performing music/singing
- going to rock concerts
- social dancing
- home improvement/repair
- battle reenactment/LARPing/cosplay
- organizing
- ping pong

- traveling by motorcycle
- horseback riding
- visiting amusement parks
- community activism
- entertaining
- acting
- frisbee golf

E. If most of your answers are E, you are a border collie. The most effective stress recovery activities are active and allow you to be distracted from things causing you stress. Exercise, highly engaging hobbies, and other activities that engage the body and brain are your best bet. Try activities such as:

- paintball
- rock climbing
- mountain climbing
- running marathons
- flying
- sailboat racing
- fencing
- adventure racing
- team sports
- skiing/snowboarding
- parkour

💜 zip-lining/bungee jumping

💜 surfing

💜 windsurfing

💜 ultimate frisbee

💜 scuba diving

Ultimately, you need to give yourself permission to make the time for activities that allow you to disengage from thoughts about the source of your stress so that your cortisol level can come down. Activities that combine disconnection and one of the strategies from Chapters 5 through 8 are especially beneficial.

What is your Stress Recovery Personality Type?

_____

Think about the type of activities you could incorporate into your day to disengage and recover from emotional stress.

Before work, what could you do to start your day disengaged from emotional stress?

_____

_____

_____

_____

_____

At mid-day, what could you do to disengage and refocus?

_____

_____

_____

_____

_____

_____

As you transition from work to home, what activities could you include?

_____

_____

_____

_____

_____

As you transition to bedtime, what type of activities will allow you to disengage from emotional stress and lower your cortisol levels for sleep?

_____

_____

_____

_____

_____

_____

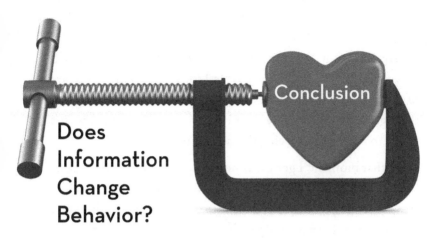

Does Information Change Behavior?

You would think that surviving a heart attack at age 35 while pregnant with twins would be enough to turn me into a workout-crazed fitness queen.

It wasn't.

I had lots of information. The doctors told me a full recovery depended on exercising 30 minutes every day, but I wasn't doing it. The information wasn't enough to change my behavior.

When the girls were about six months old, my husband, Clay, put things in perspective. He was concerned about my rather lackluster efforts at exercise and told me I needed to do better. He was right, but I wasn't motivated. Too many other things needed my attention (and frankly, I just didn't feel like exercising). He was having none of it. Looking me in the eye one day, he said, "Honey, nothing else you do makes any difference to the girls and me unless you are here. You are our whole world. You need to do the work to be sure you are still around."

That certainly brought clarity. If I didn't take care of myself, how could I take care of the people I loved? If I didn't take care of myself, how would I be part of their future? We struggled through years of infertility treatments to get these girls; I wasn't about to miss out on seeing them grow up.

In that moment, I got it. It's not about a number on a scale or the size of a pair of pants. It's about maintaining a body healthy enough to get you where you want to go. The price of admission to the future I want with my husband, daughters, and future grandchildren is moving around 30 minutes every day, managing my risk factors, and controlling my stress. It is a small price I'm happy to pay—as long as I remember why I'm doing it.

How do you find the motivation to exercise and make healthy choices every day? The risk of disease sometime in the future isn't very motivating. Truth be told, we are far more motivated by what we value than by what we fear. Denial takes over, and you can easily push away warnings of illness or death. Connecting your health with being able to share in the things you value will make the difference.

A stress-proof heart is strong enough to get you to the moments you don't want to miss. How can you focus on those moments to keep yourself motivated to do the stress-proofing work?

Creating an "I will because" statement connects the strategies you have identified to process the cortisol out of your system and protect your heart with the motivation of the moments you are unwilling to miss.

We all find our motivation in different moments. Choosing one strategy for 90 days and connecting it to a specific moment you don't want to miss is the key to successful stress-proofing. You don't have to change everything all at once.

How will you commit to something specific and achievable?

Over the years, I've heard many people make their "I will because" commitments. Some stand out in my memory:

- ♥ I will choose a colorful lunch because I want to see my granddaughter get married.

- ♥ I will go to sleep the same day I woke up because I want to make it home safely from work and not doze off behind the wheel.

- ♥ I will train and run a 5K race because I want to keep up with my wife on the golf course.

- ♥ In the next 90 days, I will change my breath when I feel stress from my schedule or traffic ramping up because I want to celebrate my 30th birthday in Las Vegas.

- ♥ I will take care of myself first—exercise in the morning and pay attention to the signs of stress— because I want to be the first woman in my family to live longer than 60 years.

- ♥ I will sing at the top of my lungs before I get out of the car to go into work because I want to see my team through this change.

What moment are you unwilling to miss?

💜 Is there a graduation, wedding, birth, anniversary, or other event you don't want to miss?

💜 Do you imagine spending your retirement on the golf course, on a sailboat, or in your garden?

💜 Do you long to see the Great Wall or some other exotic place?

💜 Is there something you've always wanted to try or experience?

My moment:

_____

Write your "I will because" statement:

I will

_____

Because I want

_____

Don't get caught up in perfection

As I tell my clients, "Life is not about perfection. It's about moving in the right direction." There are days I take a step off the path, when I let stress get the better of me or eat cookies instead of lunch. If you stumble when trying to meet your goal, don't beat yourself up. If you miss a day, don't abandon your new healthy habit; start again the next day. You'll make it.

My goal with this book is to provide tools to help you along your own path. Know I'm working and stumbling along my path to maintaining a stress-proof heart right along with you. Come share your journey and "I will because" statements at IwillBecause .com or on social media with the hashtag #IWillBecause. You can find more tips and articles and ask questions on my blog: EmbraceYourHeart.com.

May your stress-proof heart carry you to all of the moments you look forward to experiencing. I wish you a lifetime of low stress and great success!

STRESS-PROOF
── *your* ──
LIFE

Miranda looked down at her bare leg peeking out from the examination gown as she waited for the doctor. She'd been so tired lately, which isn't surprising. As managing editor for a start-up news website, Miranda was working long hours under intense pressure. She'd also been achy, which probably meant she caught whatever her assistant's kids were sick with last week. Now, however, there is a weird rash on her leg. She came to the doctor thinking the dogs gave her poison ivy, but she was wrong.

She is only 34—how can she possibly have shingles? Isn't that an old person's disease? The doctor isn't surprised, however. She tells Miranda that the pace at which she's been working is putting too much pressure on her body and has weakened her immune system as a result. There is a vaccine now for shingles. Too bad there isn't a vaccine to make her immune to stress!

Becoming immune to stress

Much like a flu shot can prevent or lessen the impact of influenza, becoming stress-proof means building an immunity to stressors you cannot avoid. Stress-proofing is a multi-pronged approach to developing immunity to stress and it starts by figuring out the source of stress. The key to developing a vaccine is isolating the cause of a disease. The first key to becoming immune to stress is clearly identifying the cause.

What is really causing all of that stress?

Rarely a day goes by without a news story or social media post about work-life balance, or the lack of it. Unrelenting job stress has been declared a global epidemic by the United Nations and is the leading cause of stress for all Americans. Caring for children or elders, arguing with a colleague, or having a leaky roof can be stressful, but chronic high stress—the kind that kills—is caused by overwhelm and uncertainty. How do I know?

In the research I've conducted on job stress, only 7 percent of the more than 4,000 people participating in my study rated work-life balance issues as one of the top factors causing stress.

Work-life balance strategies try to solve the wrong problem. For example, low staff levels cause stress because employees have to take on additional work and worry their evaluation will suffer. No amount of deep breathing will resolve that situation. Unfortunately, for most of us, the issues of overwhelm,

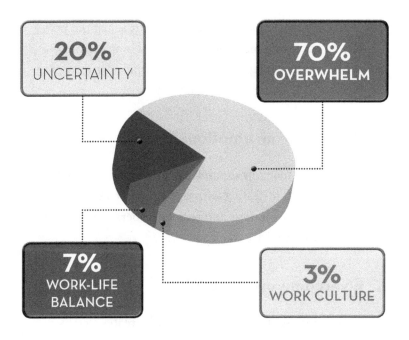

20% UNCERTAINTY

70% OVERWHELM

7% WORK-LIFE BALANCE

3% WORK CULTURE

uncertainty, and contagious stress are outside of our control—which is why we need to become immune to it. It is time to treat stress management as a HARD SKILL that is essential to success and a high quality of life. It is time to become stress-proof so that you can perform under pressure rather than being bogged down by it.

Build immunity to stress using four principles:

1. Offset the physical impact of stress

Stress-Proof Your Heart focuses on dealing with the burden that stress can put on your physical and emotional health.

Offsetting this impact is essential, and it is just the first step to becoming immune to unavoidable stress. *Stress-Proof Your Life* integrates this concept into the workplace to support well-being and productivity.

2. Recover from emotional stress

Stress-Proof Your Life expands on the emotional toll of stress to include dealing with contagious stress from others and how leaders and team members can use this information to drive more success.

3. Overcome overwhelm

One insidious effect of stress is that it creates a crisis of urgency. Every commitment, task, relationship, and obligation screams for your attention at the same volume, making it hard to discern what's important or how to feel successful. Unique stress-proof exercises quiet the cry of swirling overwhelm so that it becomes possible to focus on what's most important and then use that focus to improve quality of life and performance.

4. Combat uncertainty

Under stress, our brains depend on instinct rather than rational thought because the part of the brain responsible for critical thinking is busy dealing with the emotional reaction to stress. This reaction not only impedes productivity, but it also creates a paralyzing loop of anxiety. The principles shared in *Stress-Proof Your Life* provide a strategic system to manufacture the security necessary to live and work well.

Insight for teams, leaders, and organizations

My research has been a back-stage pass to see how high performance, purpose-driven organizations create cultures that are immune to overwhelm and uncertainty. I received volumes of unvarnished truth from the participants in my study. I've seen what works and what doesn't. My new book provides ways to:

- Uncover hidden causes of stress and institutional blind spots
- Analyze the impact of stress on culture, engagement, purpose-driven benefits, and risk management
- Improve morale, productivity, innovation, recruitment, and retention
- Create recovery, security, and growth-focused reward, benefit, and wellness programs
- Manage generations in the workforce
- Weather crisis and change
- Create artifacts of growth to drive success and connect with organizational purpose

Are you ready to live and work well under pressure?

Learn more in Eliz Greene's *Stress-Proof Your Life.*

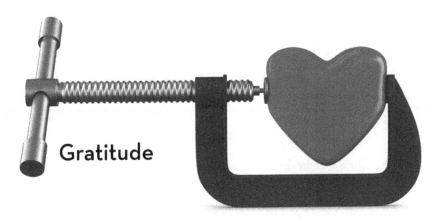

Gratitude

First, thanks for reading this section! Most people breeze past the acknowledgment section of the book, so I am grateful to you.

Some people say my speeches often sound like a love letter to my husband. They should. Clay is my biggest fan, and I am beyond grateful for his love, support, and ability to bring me back to reality with well-timed sarcasm. If you think I said or wrote something funny, it is likely he said it first.

Our daughters say they gave me my job. They did. I am grateful for every day I get to be their mother (some days more grateful than others). I can't wait to see what they do next.

If the key to success is surrounding yourself with people who inspire and push you...well, then my key to success has been joining the National Speakers Association. My fellow members have supported me—and kicked me into gear. On this project, I'm grateful to:

💜 Jess Pettitt, Thom Singer, and Gerry O'Brion are more than my mastermind group—they are my chosen family. Thanks for refusing to let me quit.

💜 Michele Payn asks hard questions. Thank you for inviting me to share your book journey and shepherding mine.

💜 Lisa Haen never lets me hide. Thank you for late-night conversation and day-time strategy.

💜 Chris Clarke-Epstein sets the standard for being an author and speaker. Thank you for leading the way.

💜 Mellanie True Hills uses her story to change the world. Thank you for being my heart-sister.

💜 Sam Silverstein reached out to tell me it is time to step up. Thank you for introducing me to Sound Wisdom and for encouraging me.

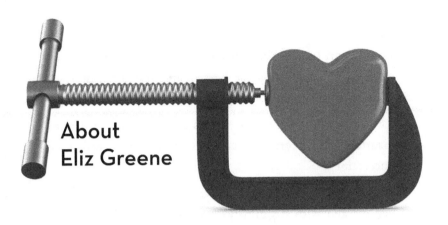

About
Eliz Greene

Eliz Greene is ridiculously excited about stress. She not only finds the chemical reaction in the body caused by stress fascinating, but stress is also her favorite topic to speak about, write about, or discuss in line at the grocery store.

With a surgically repaired heart, Eliz also knows stress management isn't a "nice-to-have," but rather an essential, survival skill. Surviving a heart attack at age 35 while seven months pregnant with twins propelled Eliz on a mission to share her story to inspire other busy people to pay attention to their health.

Just days after her heart stopped and she endured open-heart surgery and a cesarean delivery, Eliz held both her daughters together for the first time. Amazingly, despite the pain and uncertainty, what she felt most strongly was contentment. Her priorities were crystal clear. She knew she'd been given a second chance at life and a unique perspective for a reason.

For nearly two decades Eliz Greene has traveled the country sharing her story and down-to-earth, well-researched methods to improve heart health. She honed practical and implementable strategies to manage stress for herself and the thousands of audience members and readers she reaches each year.

Her research uncovered the secrets of how purpose-driven organizations create corporate cultures immune to overwhelm and uncertainty.

As a keynote speaker and worksite wellness consultant, she has worked with organizations such as NASA, Colgate-Palmolive Company, Kowa Pharmaceuticals America, United Parcel Service, Nationwide Mutual Insurance Company, Merck, Boston Scientific, WE Energies, IEWC Global Solutions, South Dakota Public Health Department, Society of Women Engineers, Association of Women Lawyers, and the American Heart Association. She was chosen to represent the future of the speaking industry by the National Speakers Association at its 40th anniversary and has presented numerous times on the business of speaking.

She's been profiled on CNN, PBS, Lifetime, TNT, and has been interviewed on countless national and local news programs.

Eliz is a seasoned spokesperson for campaigns such as the American Heart Association's Go Red For Women initiative and the Take Cholesterol to Heart campaign, a joint initiative of Regis Philbin, Howie Mandel, the American Academy of Family Physicians Foundation, and Kowa Pharmaceuticals America. Public relations and advertising agencies leverage her speaking platform and social media standing to advance their messages through traditional and earned media.

The American Heart Association presented Eliz with the Heart Hero Award in 2010 for her work in advocating for the HEART for Women Act, lobbying Congress, raising awareness, and educating healthcare professionals on the unique needs of women with heart disease.

Eliz is an author and writes a top health and wellness blog. She was named as a Top Online Influencer on stress and heart health. She has been recognized as a medically ethical blogger for providing well-researched and responsible information.

She holds a degree in communications from the University of Wisconsin–Madison with a focus on research. In order to provide scientifically relevant data on job stress, she worked with a professor emeritus from the University of Wisconsin–Madison to develop the research study.

Eliz is a leader in the speaker profession. She led the National Speakers Association's Academy for new speakers at both the national and chapter levels for more than a decade. She has been on several strategic task forces during times of transition and has led two dynamic diversity groups within the organization.

In addition to her degree in communications, Eliz is also trained as an adaptive movement specialist, dance teacher, and choreographer. She uses her adaptive training to create implementable strategies for health and stress management for people of all needs and challenges.

An avid sailor, Eliz enjoys time on Lake Michigan with her husband, Clay, and their beautiful (now 18-year-old) daughters.

Connect with Eliz Greene

Hire Eliz to speak at your event or train your leaders & employees:

Reach out to our team:

www.ElizGreene.com

Kate@ElizGreene.com

414-207-6878

Visit Eliz's Blog:

www.EmbraceYourHeart.com

Join Eliz's Page on Facebook:

www.facebook.com/elizgreenespeaker/

Connect with Eliz on LinkedIn:

www.linkedin.com/in/elizgreene/

Subscribe to Eliz's YouTube channel:

www.youtube.com/elizgreene/

Check out the latest Stress-Proof products:

www.StressProofBook.com

Leave your comments and intentions:

www.iWillBecause.com